SPECTRUM®
READERS

LEVEL **1**

AWESOME!
Snakes

By Teresa Domnauer

Carson-Dellosa
Publishing

An imprint of Carson-Dellosa Publishing, LLC
P.O. Box 35665
Greensboro, NC 27425-5665

carsondellosa.com

Printed in the USA. All rights reserved.
ISBN 978-1-62399-137-1

01-002131120

They slither.
They crawl.
They climb trees.
They hunt and swim.
Warning: amazing snakes
ahead!

Egyptian Cobra

Snakes can curl into a circle.
Scales cover their bodies.

Green Viper

Snakes have tongues that look like forks.
Their tongues help them smell enemies and find food.

Rattlesnake

Snakes have special ways
to stay safe.
This snake shakes its tail.
The sound tells enemies
to stay away.

Black Cobra

This snake lifts up its body
to look bigger.
This keeps away some
of its enemies.

Emerald Tree Boa

Some snakes can climb trees. This snake's color helps it hide in the leaves.

Burmese Python

Some snakes live in warm places.
This snake lives in a tropical rain forest.

Sand Viper

Some snakes live in hot deserts.
This snake hides in the desert sand.

Yellow-Lip Sea Snake

Other snakes live in
the ocean.
This snake has a flat tail.
Its tail helps it paddle
through water.

Copperhead

Snakes hunt for food.

Natal Green Snake

Some snakes, like this one,
hunt at night.
They rest during the day.

King Brown Snake

Snakes live all over
the world.
This snake lives in Australia.

Green Mamba

This snake lives in Africa.
It has a very dangerous bite.
Poison, called *venom*, comes
out of its fangs.

Spitting Cobra

This snake has dangerous venom, too.
It can spit the venom over six feet.

Milk Snake

This snake is not harmful at all.
But enemies stay away from it.
It looks just like a dangerous snake.

AWESOME! Snakes
Comprehension Questions

1. How do snakes use their tongues?

2. What does it mean when a rattlesnake shakes its tail?

3. Why does the black cobra lift up its body?

4. Where does the Burmese python live?

5. Why does the yellow-lip sea snake have a flat tail?

6. How does a snake eat its food?

7. Where does the king brown snake live?

8. Do you think you would like to see a green mamba in the wild? Why or why not?

9. What is venom? Name two snakes that have venom.